Stations of the Cross
For Kids

"If any man would come after me, let him take up his cross daily and follow
Luke 9:23

Let us follow our dear Lord Jesus ashe travels the Way of the Cross. He is asking us to follow him.

Are you afraid?

Jesus himself was afraid to walk this painful journey, but out of love for us, he did so. So for love of him, we will follow.

How do we pick up our cross and follow him? By putting up with the suffering, little or big, in our own lives: not being able to do what we want, people not understanding us, sickness, hardship, pain, or even boredom. When we do this patiently and cheerfully, we are following him. And we can remember his way of the Cross, which was so hard and so painful.

As he walked to suffer and die for us, so many people were unaware of what he was doing. Or perhaps they knew but decided not to watch. All these went on their way, playing, stealing, working, complaining, ignoring. Only a few people were brave enough to go with him: his mother Mary, his apostle John, and Mary Magdalene, and some others we will meet.

Let us go with them now, and with Jesus. It is the little we can do to show our love for him.

Within each station, you will find the following:

Each station has a street scene with many people. Try to follow Christ and his Mother on their way to Golgotha. Notice what the other people are doing. Who is helping Jesus? Who is hurting him? Who is not paying attention? What sorts of things are they doing? How are the things they are doing related to what is happening to Jesus? See the boy and girl in the top corner stealing apples from their neighbor's tree. How is their story part of Jesus's story?

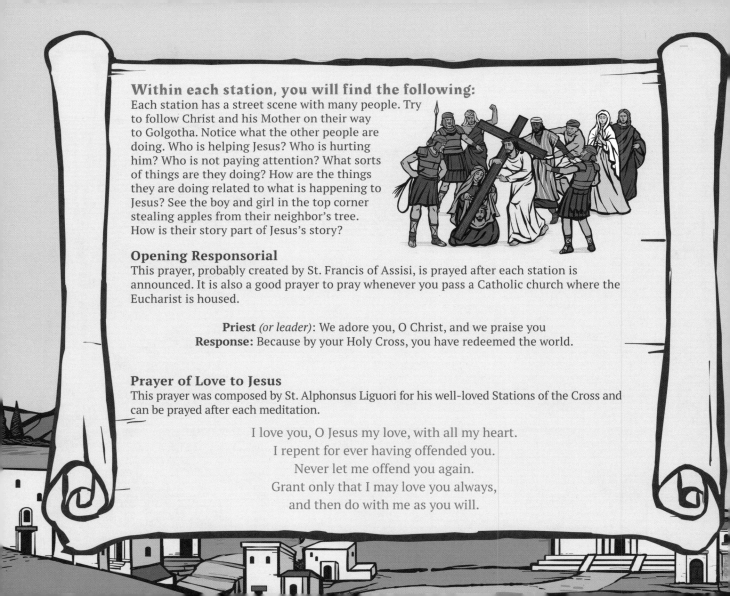

Opening Responsorial

This prayer, probably created by St. Francis of Assisi, is prayed after each station is announced. It is also a good prayer to pray whenever you pass a Catholic church where the Eucharist is housed.

Priest *(or leader)*: We adore you, O Christ, and we praise you
Response: Because by your Holy Cross, you have redeemed the world.

Prayer of Love to Jesus

This prayer was composed by St. Alphonsus Liguori for his well-loved Stations of the Cross and can be prayed after each meditation.

I love you, O Jesus my love, with all my heart.
I repent for ever having offended you.
Never let me offend you again.
Grant only that I may love you always,
and then do with me as you will.

Stations
of the
Cross

For Kids

Written by Regina Doman
Illustrated by Chris Lewis

Cover design by Chris Lewis
Illustrations by Chris Lewis

ISBN: 978-1-5051-1857-5
Kindle ISBN: 978-1-5051-1858-2
ePub ISBN: 978-1-5051-1859-9

Published in the United States by
TAN Books
PO Box 269
Gastonia, NC 28053
www.TANBooks.com
Printed in the United States of America

Look for the Flowers
These little flowers remind you to pray an
Our Father, Hail Mary, and Gloria after each Station.

Our Father, who art in heaven, hallowed be thy Name! Thy kingdom come, thy will be done on earth as it is in heaven. Give us this day our daily bread, and forgive us our trespasses as we forgive those who trespass against us, and lead us not into temptation, but deliver us from evil. Amen.

Hail Mary, full of grace! The Lord is with thee! Blessed art thou among women, and blessed is the fruit of thy womb, Jesus. Holy Mary, Mother of God, pray for us sinners now and at the hour of our death. Amen.

Glory be to the Father and to the Son and to the Holy Spirit as it was in the beginning, is now, and ever shall be, world without end. Amen.

Stabat Mater
This thirteenth-century Latin hymn to Our Lady describes how the mother of Jesus stood beside the cross (Jn 19:26) and suffered with her Son. The first of its twenty verses is traditionally sung after the opening prayer and then the next verses while walking from one station to the next, with the final verses sung at the end of the journey. You will find the verses in English and Latin at the top and bottom of the left-hand pages.

**At the cross, her station keeping,
stood the mournful Mother weeping,
close to Jesus to the last.**

Stabat Mater dolorosa iuxta crucem lacrimosa dum pendebat Filius.

Learning More
On each station, this sidebar will have more details about aspects of Christ's passion.

Where did the Stations of the Cross come from?

In Jerusalem, pilgrims still walk the route that Jesus is said to have walked, stopping at houses and chapels along the way to think about the suffering Christ endured for us. Those of us who cannot travel to Jerusalem often do the Stations of the Cross in our parish church, or even in our own homes. Walking, standing, and kneeling are important positions when praying the Stations, reminding us of Jesus's slow and painful journey up the hill to die on the Cross. Use your imagination as you think of what Jesus saw and what he suffered on the way to Calvary.

The First Station
Jesus is condemned to death

We adore you, O Christ, and we praise you, because by your Holy Cross, you have redeemed the world.

> *"Pilate, wishing to satisfy the crowd, released for them Barabbas; and having scourged Jesus, he delivered him to be crucified."*
>
> Mark 15:15

Pilate, the governor of Judea, was afraid. He did not want Jesus to die, and he could have saved him. Pilate knew that Jesus had done nothing wrong. But he was too afraid of what might happen if he set this prisoner free: riots, threats, and the loss of his job, or worse, his life. So he washed his hands to show he would stand aside as an innocent man died.

Lord, give me the courage never to betray you! Give me the strength to follow you always!

I love you, O Jesus my love, with all my heart.
I repent for ever having offended you.
Never let me offend you again.
Grant only that I may love you always,
and then do with me as you will.

**Through her heart, his sorrow sharing,
all his bitter anguish bearing,
now at length the sword had passed.**

Cuius animam gementem contristatam et dolentem pertransivit gladius.

Gabbatha: The Stone Pavement

"When Pilate heard these words, he brought Jesus out and sat down on the judgment seat at a place called The Pavement, and in Hebrew, Gabbatha" (Jn 19:13). Where was Gabbatha, the place where Pilate condemned Jesus? For many years, it was thought that Pontius Pilate, must have questioned Jesus at the Antonian fortress. This was a tower close to the Temple, which was built by Herod the Great in honor of his patron, Marc Antony. But early historians wrote that the governor stayed in Herod's palace on the western hill whenever he was in Jerusalem and used the pavement outside for judging criminals. Recent archeology has uncovered a pavement outside of Herod's palace which fits their description of the praetorium used by Pilate.

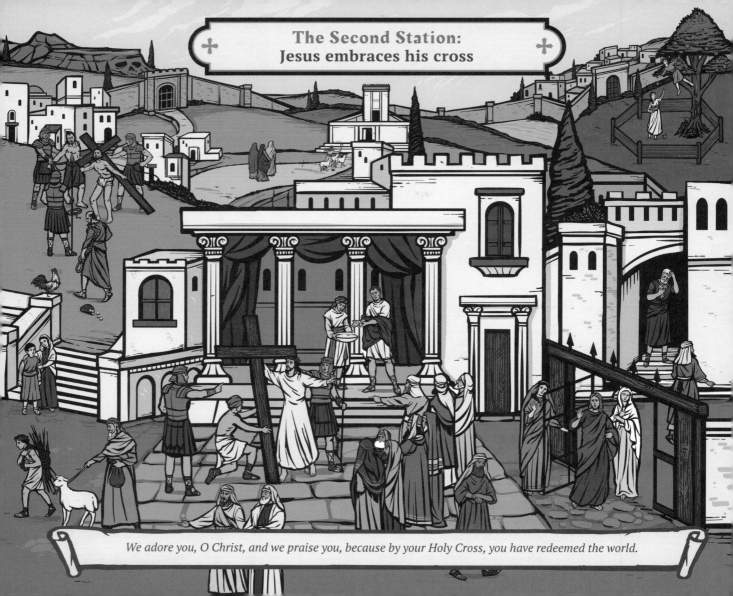

The Second Station:
Jesus embraces his cross

We adore you, O Christ, and we praise you, because by your Holy Cross, you have redeemed the world.

"So they took Jesus, and he went out, bearing his own cross."
John 19:17

If something difficult or painful needs to be done, we often want to run away from it. Jesus did not do this.

He knew he had come into this world to suffer a painful and terrifying death for us. When the time came, he did not run away. He picked up the heavy cross they were going to use to kill him and carried it. He knew this was want he had to do.

Lord, help us to carry our crosses, even the little ones, without hesitating and without complaining.

I love you, O Jesus my love, with all my heart.
I repent for ever having offended you.
Never let me offend you again.
Grant only that I may love you always,
and then do with me as you will.

**Oh how sad and sore distressed
was that mother highly blessed,
of the sole-begotten One!**

O quam tristis et afflicta fuit illa benedicta Mater Unigeniti!

The Relic of the True Cross

Nearly 350 years after Christ died, Emperor Constantine halted the persecution of Christians. His devout mother, Helen, traveled to Israel around AD 326 to visit the place where Christ had been crucified. The Romans had built a pagan temple there, which she had pulled down. There they discovered three crosses buried in the ground, and the bishop of Jerusalem suggested having each of the crosses touched to a dying woman. When the third cross touched the invalid, she was instantly cured, and that cross was given a place of honor in the church Helen built over Christ's empty tomb, the Church of the Holy Sepulcher. A nun who visited the church in AD 380 wrote of how the wood of the True Cross was venerated by the faithful on Good Friday, much as Catholics do today with their parish crucifix. Nearly 98 percent of the True Cross was lost or destroyed in the Muslim conquest of the Holy Land, but some highly treasured fragments are still venerated today.

The Third Station:
Jesus falls the first time

We adore you, O Christ, and we praise you, because by your Holy Cross, you have redeemed the world.

"Surely he has borne our griefs and carried our sorrows."
Isaiah 53:4

Have you ever decided to carry your cross without complaining and failed? Have you ever set out to do good, or even just do your part, and given up?

Do not be sad or discouraged! Jesus also stumbled while carrying his cross. He fell, crushed beneath its weight. Others probably laughed at him. But Jesus stood up, picked up his cross again, and kept going.

Lord, give us the courage to rise to our feet if ever we fall beneath the weight of our cross!

I love you, O Jesus my love, with all my heart.
I repent for ever having offended you.
Never let me offend you again.
Grant only that I may love you always,
and then do with me as you will.

**Christ above in torment hangs;
she beneath beholds the pangs
of her dying glorious Son.**

Quae moerebat et dolebat et tremebat cum videbat nati poenas incliti

The Prophet Isaiah and the Suffering Servant

Nearly seven hundred years before Christ, the prophet Isaiah, who lived during the reign of King Hezekiah of Jerusalem, prophesied that a servant of God would suffer a cruel death. This servant, who was specially chosen by God and would be called his Son, would be sentenced to an unjust death, mocked, and scourged. He would die bearing the heavy burden of all our sins. Isaiah describes this suffering servant as "bruised," "crushed," "despised," and "through his wounds, we are healed." This prophecy was recorded in the Book of Isaiah, the first of the prophetic books in the Bible. During Lent, the Church meditates on the details of this most remarkable Scripture. Verses of this prophecy are used in this book for some stations.

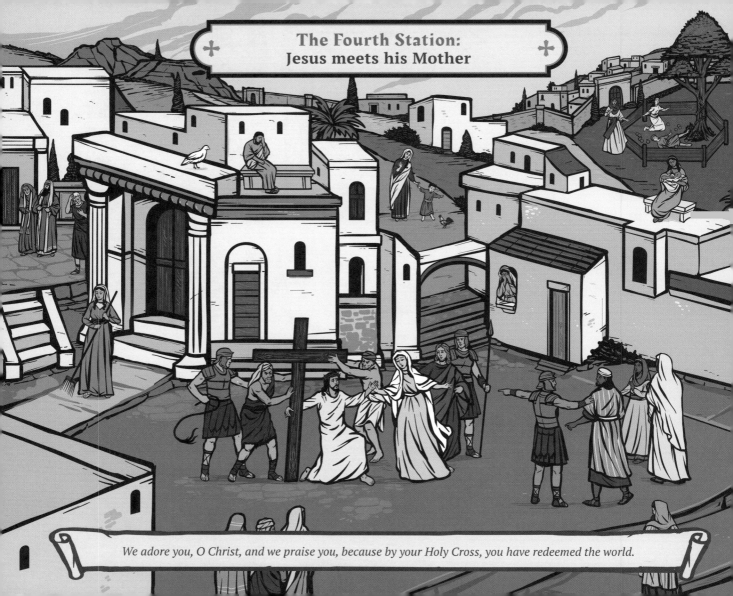

The Fourth Station:
Jesus meets his Mother

We adore you, O Christ, and we praise you, because by your Holy Cross, you have redeemed the world.

> *"This child is destined for the falling and the rising of many in Israel, and to be a sign that will be opposed so that the inner thoughts of many will be revealed—and a sword will pierce your own soul too."*
> Luke 2:34–35 NRSV

O Mary! When Jesus was a small child, you must have picked him up so many times when he fell and got hurt. You were always there to make things better, as mothers do. But now you cannot help Jesus or stop others from hurting him. There is nothing you can do to take away the pain. But still you go to meet him, to be with him and share in his sufferings. And this you do for us as well, whenever we are in pain or when we are sad.

O Mary, who suffered alongside your Son, teach us to love him as you do, and come to our side when we suffer.

I love you, O Jesus my love, with all my heart.
I repent for ever having offended you.
Never let me offend you again.
Grant only that I may love you always,
and then do with me as you will.

**Is there one who would not weep,
whelmed in miseries so deep
Christ's dear Mother to behold?**

Quis est homo qui non fleret Matri Christi si videret in tanto supplicio?

Our Lady of Sorrows

The prophet Simeon met Our Lady in the Temple as she brought baby Jesus to present him to the Lord, telling her, "A sword will pierce your own soul also" (Lk 2:35). Catholics honor Our Lady with the title "Our Lady of Sorrows," and in AD 1232, seven young men founded a religious order, the Servites, to meditate on seven sorrowful moments in her life. These include Simeon's prophecy, the flight into Egypt, losing the child Jesus in the Temple, the Way of the Cross, the Crucifixion, the descent from the Cross, and his burial. Artistically, each of these sorrows is depicted as a sword piercing the Immaculate Heart of Mary. In troubled times, we can always take comfort in knowing Our Lady understands sorrow so well.

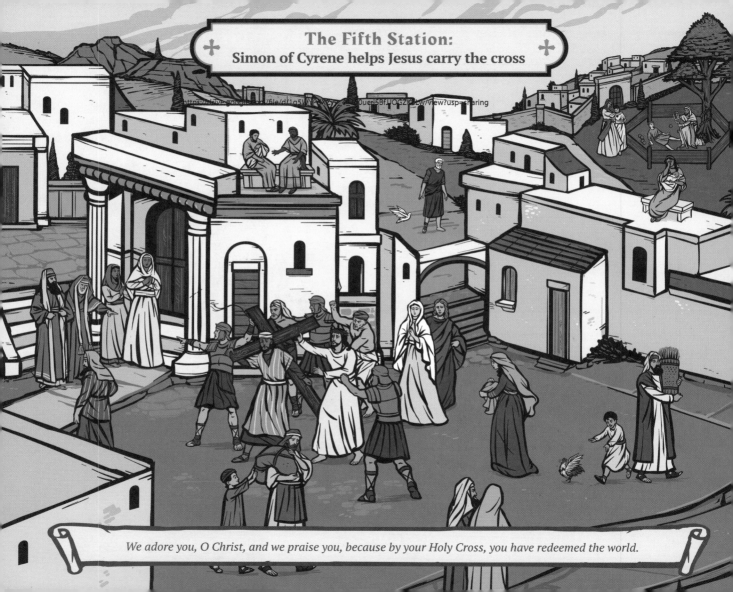

The Fifth Station:
Simon of Cyrene helps Jesus carry the cross

We adore you, O Christ, and we praise you, because by your Holy Cross, you have redeemed the world.

"As they led him away, they seized one Simon of Cyrene, who was coming in from the country, and laid on him the cross, to carry it behind Jesus."
Luke 23:26

Did you notice that nearly all the stations so far begin with the word "Jesus"? But not this one. Why? Because Simon can stand as a symbol for all of us. We, too, can help Jesus carry his cross by bearing our own suffering patiently and by helping others who are suffering. Simon did not choose to help Jesus at first; rather, he was forced to. In the same way, many times we do not choose to suffer: it is forced on us by sickness, accident, or unfair treatment. But when it comes, can we be like Simon, compassionate and supportive of others? Can we join in helping Christ with the great work of redemption?

O Lord Jesus, give me the strength and compassion to be like Simon by helping others carry their crosses.

I love you, O Jesus my love, with all my heart.
I repent for ever having offended you.
Never let me offend you again.
Grant only that I may love you always,
and then do with me as you will.

**Can the human heart refrain
from partaking in her pain,
in that Mother's pain untold?**

Quis non posset contristari Matrem Christi contemplari dolentum cum filio?

Simon of Cyrene

Simon, sometimes called St. Simon the Cyrenian, was thought to be a Jew or a Jewish convert from the city of Cyrene in North Africa. After carrying the cross of Jesus, tradition says he and his family became Christians. Mark mentions in his Gospel that Simon was "the father of Alexander and Rufus" (Mk 15:21), and St. Paul later sends greetings to Rufus and his mother in Romans 16:13. Simon and his family may be the "Cyrenian men" who evangelized the Greek-speaking Jews in Acts (11:20). Like many early saints, Simon was never officially canonized, but Christians throughout the centuries have honored him and invoked him in prayer. He is called the patron saint of volunteers, helpful passersby, and those who choose to "bear one another's burdens" (Gal 6:2).

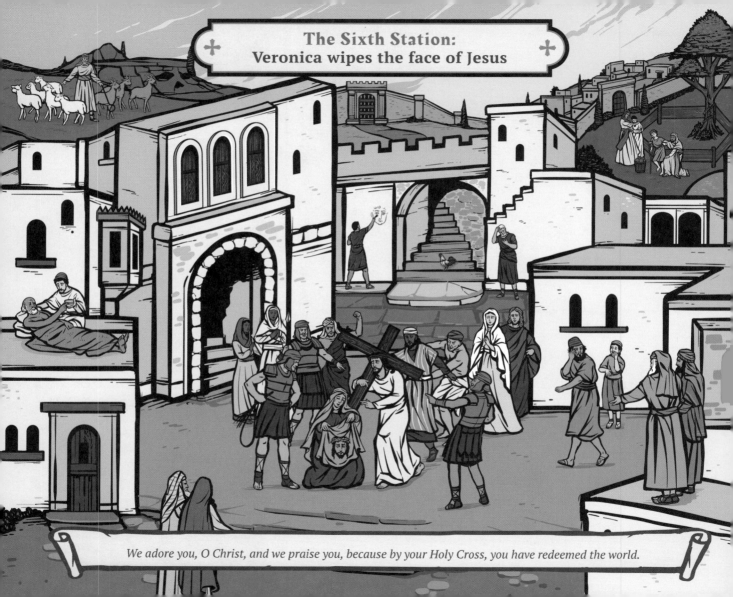

The Sixth Station:
Veronica wipes the face of Jesus

We adore you, O Christ, and we praise you, because by your Holy Cross, you have redeemed the world.

"As many were astonished at Him—
His appearance was so marred, beyond human semblance,
and His form beyond that of the sons of men."
Isaiah 52:14

This is the other station which does not start with the name of Jesus but with another name, Veronica, which means, "true image." She, too, helps Jesus, not by carrying the cross but by wiping His face of its blood and sweat, something He could not do for Himself while carrying the cross. It is a small thing but it takes courage, and Jesus is so grateful that He leaves an image of His face on her veil which Christians would later marvel at. See how Jesus rewards even a small, quick act of love?

Lord Jesus, help us love You and others, even in small ways!

I love you, O Jesus my love, with all my heart.
I repent for ever having offended you.
Never let me offend you again.
Grant only that I may love you always,
and then do with me as you will.

For the sins of His own nation
saw Him hang in desolation,
all with bloody scourges rent.

Pro peccatis suae gentis vidit Iesum in tormentis et flagellis subditum.

Veronica's Veil

Although the story of Veronica and her veil is not found in the Gospels, fourth-century Christian writings spoke of a woman called Berenikē who was healed of a flow of blood by Jesus. Her name means "Veronica" in Latin. The Gospel of Luke does mention a woman Christ healed in a similar way. Perhaps she was one of the compassionate women who followed Him on His way to be crucified. During the Middle Ages, the story of Berenike/Veronica became associated with the "icon of Christ with No Hands" His bloodstained face depicted on a veil or cloth, which reminds us that Christ needs our hands to help others just as Veronica helped him.

The Seventh Station:
Jesus falls the second time

We adore you, O Christ, and we praise you, because by your Holy Cross, you have redeemed the world.

"But he was wounded for our transgressions,
he was bruised for our iniquities;
upon him was the chastisement that made us whole,
and with his stripes we are healed."
Isaiah 53:5

It happens again: another fall. Was the cross too heavy for Jesus? Was saving us too difficult a job for him? No. Jesus is God. Of course he could have carried the cross without falling. So why did he keep falling? Was it to teach us to be patient with ourselves when we fall? Was it to teach us to be patient with others when they fall? In that mysterious place where God and man are one in Christ Jesus, did he want to show us how he works?

If we don't know why he fell, we do know why he got back up, shouldered the cross once again, and kept walking to his death: out of love for us; for me and for you.

Lord, help us to always trust in you!

I love you, O Jesus my love, with all my heart.
I repent for ever having offended you.
Never let me offend you again.
Grant only that I may love you always,
and then do with me as you will.

Bruised, derided, cursed, defiled,
she beheld her tender child,
till his Spirit forth he sent.

Vidit suum dulcem natum moriendo desolatum dum emisit spiritum.

The Precious Blood of Christ

At the first Passover, God directed the Israelites to put the blood of a sacrificed lamb on their doorposts to shield their firstborn from the Angel of Death. Later, the Jewish high priest would enter the Holy of Holies on the Day of Atonement to sprinkle the blood of sacrificed animals in reparation for the sins of the people. At the Last Supper, Christ took a cup of wine, gave it to his disciples, and said, "Drink of it, all of you; for this is my blood of the covenant, which is poured out for many for the forgiveness of sins" (Mt 26:27–28). This, with his death on the Cross, combined the Passover with the Atonement Sacrifice to become one perfect sacrifice. Pope St. Clement I wrote in AD 96: "Let us fix our gaze on the Blood of Christ and realize how truly precious It is, seeing that It was poured out for our salvation and brought the grace of conversion to the whole world."

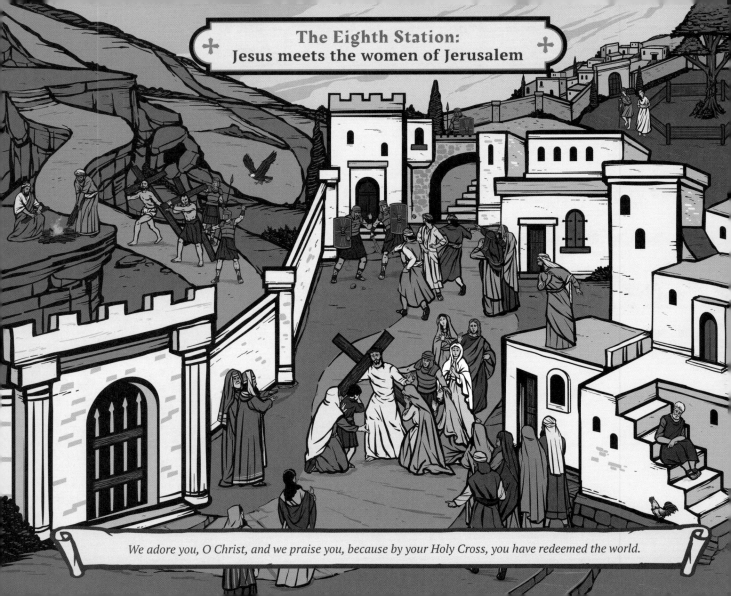

The Eighth Station:
Jesus meets the women of Jerusalem

We adore you, O Christ, and we praise you, because by your Holy Cross, you have redeemed the world.

> *"And there followed him a great multitude of the people, and of women who bewailed and lamented him. But Jesus turning to them said, 'Daughters of Jerusalem, do not weep for me, but weep for yourselves and for your children.'"*
> Luke 23:27–28, 31

The women wail when they see Jesus going to his death. They loved to hear him teach and marveled at his healing powers. They loved how he blessed their children, who had praised him as the Son of David. Could he be the Messiah who would restore the kingdom of Israel? Now Jesus is on his way to die, and they weep for their dreams and their children's dreams. But Jesus comforts them and instead urges them to repent and pray for themselves and for their children.

Lord, help me to remember the sufferings of others even when I suffer. May I weep with the women of Jerusalem for all those who suffer, and most of all, for the pain which our sins cause you. For sin is worse than death.

I love you, O Jesus my love, with all my heart.
I repent for ever having offended you.
Never let me offend you again.
Grant only that I may love you always,
and then do with me as you will.

**O, thou Mother, fount of love,
touch my spirit from above,
make my heart with thine accord.**

Eia Mater, fons amoris, me sentire vim doloris fac ut tecum lugeam.

The Destruction of Jerusalem

Shortly before he died, Jesus warned his apostles that if men would not repent, Jerusalem and the Temple would be utterly destroyed: "This generation will not pass away till all these things take place" (Mt 24:34). Jesus's words did indeed come true. When the children of the mothers who had seen Jesus die were old, Roman armies surrounded the city of Jerusalem. Tradition says that those who remembered Christ's warning fled the city while there was still time. While warring factions of Jewish leaders fought one another, most of the people in the city starved to death, the city was burned to the ground and even the stones of the Temple were thrown down and carted off to make other buildings. The Jewish people mourn the loss of the Temple yearly on Tisha B'Av, a day of fasting.

The Ninth Station:
Jesus falls the third time

We adore you, O Christ, and we praise you, because by your Holy Cross, you have redeemed the world.

> *"All we like sheep have gone astray, each one turning to his own way, and the Lord has laid upon him the iniquity of us all."*
>
> *Isaiah 53:6*

Are you still following Jesus? Look, he has fallen again. Why does he keep falling? Is he not the Lion of Judah? The King of kings? The Mighty Lord? Why is this so hard for him? Are we making it hard for him? Yes, we do, whenever we fail to carry our crosses, whenever we hurt others or ourselves, whenever we sin. All this makes his cross heavier. This fall reminds us: our sins hurt Jesus. They make him fall. But he carries them. He gets up and keeps carrying them because he loves us. Our sins cannot stop him from loving us.

Lord, thank you for your love for me! Help me live my life for you alone!

I love you, O Jesus my love, with all my heart.
I repent for ever having offended you.
Never let me offend you again.
Grant only that I may love you always,
and then do with me as you will.

**Make me feel as thou has felt;
make my soul to glow and melt
with the love of Christ our Lord.**

Fac ut ardeat cor meum in amando Christum Deum ut sibi complaceam.

The History of the Stations

From early times, Christians have longed to go to Jerusalem and visit the places where Christ walked. After Jerusalem was destroyed, Christians would visit the ruins. St. Jerome wrote that his friend and co-translator of the Vulgate Bible, St. Paula, visited sites in AD 386 such as the pillar where Christ was scourged and the tomb where he was buried. After Jerusalem was rebuilt, Christians began making pilgrimages there, and during Lent, it became customary to travel the road where Christ was thought to have carried his cross, called the Via Dolorosa or Road of Sorrow. The Stations as we know them were created around 1517 when the Franciscan order, which cared for the Roman Catholic churches in the Holy Land, marked out a path for pilgrims to follow, using markers like the one below.

The Tenth Station:
Jesus is stripped of his garments

We adore you, O Christ, and we praise you, because by your Holy Cross, you have redeemed the world.

> *"They parted my garments among them,*
> *and for my clothing they cast lots."*
> John 19:24

When Jesus was born in a stable, he was naked, as we all are when we are born. But his Mother Mary clothed him in linen and cuddled him. Now that Jesus has come to the place of execution, some traditions tell us that he is still, in this moment, wearing garments made by his Mother—a skillfully made linen tunic with no seams, like a priest's garment. The soldiers take even that away from him, ripping it off and throwing dice to see who will get to keep it. He came into the world naked, and now he will leave it naked. He gave us everything, and we took everything from him. Yet he loves us, from the beginning to the end of his life.

O Jesus, help us to love you above everything else in life. When we lose something precious, help us to love you more!

I love you, O Jesus my love, with all my heart.
I repent for ever having offended you.
Never let me offend you again.
Grant only that I may love you always,
and then do with me as you will.

Holy Mother, pierce me through;
in my heart each wound renew
of my Saviour crucified.

Sancta Mater, istud agas, crucifixi fige plagas cordi meo valide.

The Holy Coat of Christ

Several churches are thought to preserve garments worn by Christ during his lifetime. The cathedral of Sts. Peter and Helen in Trier, Germany, has a seamless garment which is thought to be the one which was taken from him right before His crucifixion. Local tradition says that St. Helen, who was born in that area, had the coat sent there. The cathedral there does indeed contain the remains of a basilica built during the time of Constantine, which makes this tradition plausible. During a ninth century invasion, the coat was sealed up in a wall of the basilica and later rediscovered in 1196. Beginning in 1513, the cathedral has held periodic displays of the coat, which is brown in color and very fragile. Since 1996, annual pilgrimages allow pilgrims to venerate the relic during a ten-day festival.

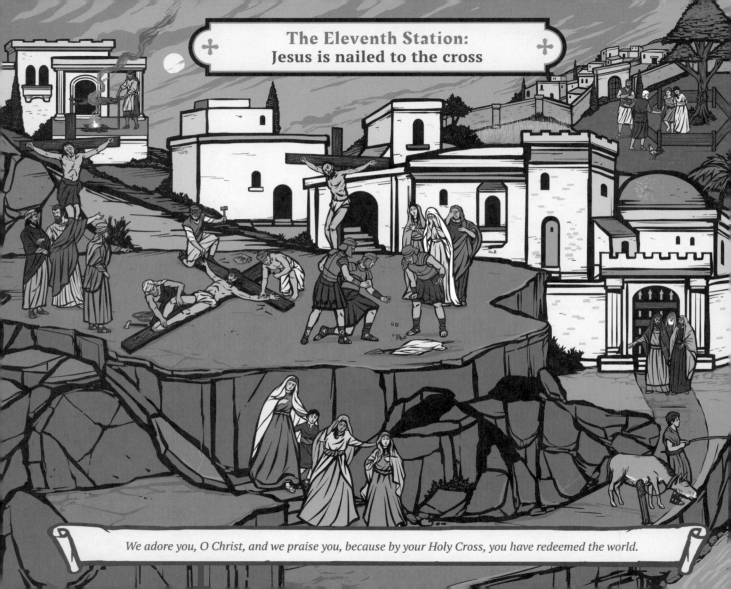

The Eleventh Station:
Jesus is nailed to the cross

We adore you, O Christ, and we praise you, because by your Holy Cross, you have redeemed the world.

"When they came to the place that is called The Skull, they crucified him, and the criminals, one on the right and one on the left. And Jesus said, "Father, forgive them; for they know not what they do."

Luke 23:33–34

This station pains us perhaps more than any other, outside of our Savior's death. The soldiers take the hands of Jesus—hands that never sinned, hands that blessed, hands that healed, hands that comforted, hands that broke bread and offered it to us as his Body—and they cruelly hammer nails through those hands, pinning them to the cross. Jesus begins his agony on the cross.

O Jesus, forgive us! Let us use our hands as you did, always to help and heal and bless and praise and to bring you to others. Forgive us. Forgive us.

I love you, O Jesus my love, with all my heart.
I repent for ever having offended you.
Never let me offend you again.
Grant only that I may love you always,
and then do with me as you will.

Let me share with thee his pain,
Who for all my sins was slain,
Who for me in torments died.

Tui nati vulnerati tam dignati pro me pati poenas mecum divide.

The Holy Nails

It is said that St. Helen found nails along with the True Cross, but how many nails there were and exactly what became of them is not entirely known. What is certain is that many Christians were eager to have one of the Holy Nails, or even part of one of them in their churches for veneration. So many of them took slivers or filings from the original nails and melded them with other nails so that the Holy Nails could be shared among different churches. Today, there are about thirty nails which may contain portions of the original nails. Some of the most famous of these relics can be found in the Basilica of the Holy Cross in Rome, in the Trier Cathedral in Germany, and in the Church of the Holy Sepulcher in Jerusalem.

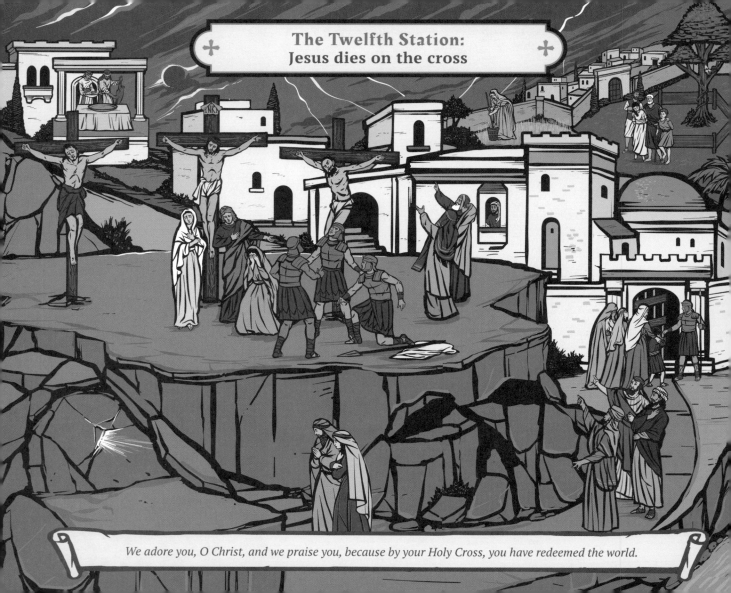

The Twelfth Station:
Jesus dies on the cross

We adore you, O Christ, and we praise you, because by your Holy Cross, you have redeemed the world.

> *"When Jesus had received the vinegar, he said, 'It is finished';*
> *and he bowed his head and gave up his spirit."*
> *John 19:30*

Jesus is dying. Only Mary and John and the Magdalene are brave enough to stay with him. Their love makes them brave. Can we stay with them? The blood of Jesus is running down the cross and trickling into the earth. That blood is redeeming Adam and Eve, Abraham and Sarah, Isaac, Jacob, Joseph, Deborah, Ruth, and David, and all the good men and women asleep in the ground, all those who have died, and all those yet to be born. His sacrifice is saving us all!

Thank you, Jesus. May we never grow tired of thanking you for your saving death.

I love you, O Jesus my love, with all my heart.
I repent for ever having offended you.
Never let me offend you again.
Grant only that I may love you always,
and then do with me as you will.

Let me mingle tears with thee,
mourning him Who mourned for me,
all the days that I may live.

Fac me vere tecum flere crucifixo condolere donec ego vixero.

Golgotha

All four Gospel writers identify the hill where Jesus was crucified as "the Place of the Skull." Some think this is because the hill was shaped like a skull, or because it was a place where criminals were executed and left to rot (leaving many skulls in the area). Or perhaps the "skull" referred to is the skull of Adam himself! Early Christian writings say that Adam, the first man, was buried beneath the Hill of Golgotha. Below the Church of the Holy Sepulcher, which stands over the spot where Christ was crucified, is a cave known as the Chapel of Adam. Tradition says that the earthquake which occurred when Christ died split the rock, causing Christ's blood to fall upon the skull of Adam, redeeming him. This is one reason why pictures of the Crucifixion sometimes have a skull at the base of the cross. What is certain is that Christ's death redeemed all humankind, from Adam down to us.

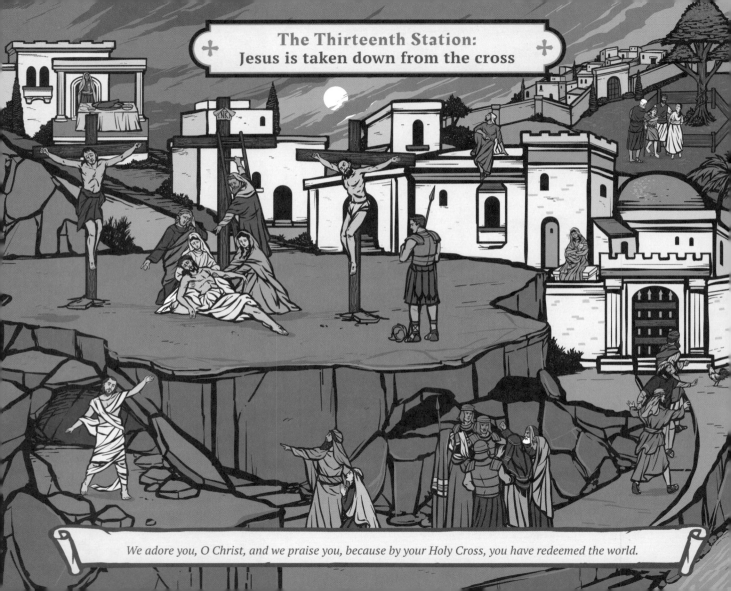

The Thirteenth Station:
Jesus is taken down from the cross

We adore you, O Christ, and we praise you, because by your Holy Cross, you have redeemed the world.

> *"Joseph of Arimathea asked for the body*
> *of Jesus. Then he took it down."*
> Luke 23:52–53

Now Jesus is taken down from the cross. His work is done, and his Body rests one more time in the arms of his blessed Mother. When he was born, Mary held him joyfully and laid him in a manger. Now she holds his crucified Body sorrowfully before she lays him in a tomb. How sad she is! But the Sabbath is coming, and the work of the burial must be started.

Too soon, Mary must surrender him again to the grave. Let us stay with her in this moment, and return to it again and again, lest we ever forget what Christ has done for us.

O Mary, pray for me!

I love you, O Jesus my love, with all my heart.
I repent for ever having offended you.
Never let me offend you again.
Grant only that I may love you always,
and then do with me as you will.

**By the cross with thee to stay,
there with thee to weep and pray,
this of thee I ask to give.**

Iuxta crucem tecum stare te libenter sociare in planctu desidero.

The Pieta

This statue of Our Lady holding the crucified body of her Son is arguably the most beautiful statue ever created, and certainly one of the most famous. Young Michelangelo Buonarotti carved it from fine white Carrara marble in 1498–99 when he was around twenty-three years old. In some places, he carved the folds of Mary's robes so thinly that light can be seen through them. The figure of Christ is perfectly life-sized, and Mary cradles him, one hand lifted in a gesture of prayer. The Pieta shows Our Lady as sorrowful but also as fully surrendered to her Son's death as she holds him one last time. Today, the statue is housed in St. Peter's Basilica in Rome where millions of visitors from all over the world come to marvel at it and pray.

**The Fourteenth Station:
Jesus is placed in the tomb**

We adore you, O Christ, and we praise you, because by your Holy Cross, you have redeemed the world.

> *"They took the body of Jesus, and bound it in linen cloths with the spices, as is the burial custom of the Jews. Now in the place where he was crucified there was a garden, and in the garden a new tomb where no one had ever been laid. So because of the Jewish day of Preparation, as the tomb was close at hand, they laid Jesus there."*
>
> *John 19:40–42*

It is done. Jesus's bloody and bruised crucified body is lovingly wrapped once more in linen bands by Mary with the help of Joseph and Nicodemus. He is laid in a cold stone tomb in a garden. From the cave of Bethlehem to the cave of the tomb, Jesus has come. His entire journey from the womb of Mary to the tomb of Joseph of Arimathea has been made with love: for love of us, for love of you and me. May we always be grateful. May we always remember the price of our lives. May this journey give us courage always to love him, and to love others as he loved us.

I love you, O Jesus my love, with all my heart.
I repent for ever having offended you.
Never let me offend you again.
Grant only that I may love you always,
and then do with me as you will.

**Virgin, of all virgins blest,
listen to my fond request:
let me share thy grief divine.**

Virgo virginum praeclara mihi iam non sis amara fac me tecum plangere.

The Shroud of Turin

One remarkable relic of Our Lord is a linen cloth said to be His burial sheet or shroud which is kept in the cathedral of Turin, Italy. It shows the image of a crucified man who has been scourged and has head wounds from a cap of thorns. Scientists debate about the age of the cloth, but none of them can explain how the image which appears on it was made. It is not painted or printed by any material known to humanity. In 1898, an Italian photographer took a picture of the shroud for the first time, and as he was developing the photo, he was shocked to see an almost sculptural image on the negative of the photograph. Since paintings do not usually produce such clear negatives, this is also unexplained. Many people see in the shroud a testament to the death and resurrection of Jesus Christ.

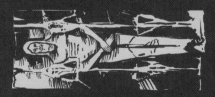

Adoramus Te, Christe, Et Benedicimus Tibi Quia Per Sanctam Crucem Tuam Redemisti Mundum.

Closing Prayers

We have finished following the way of the Cross. Jesus's journey of love for us is something we should never forget. While the pain he suffered should make us sad, the victory he won for us on the cross should make us joyful. We should never tire of marveling at what he did for us, nor should we ever fail to thank him for his sacrifice. And whenever we see him in the Eucharist, or even whenever we see a church where his Body and Blood is sheltered in the tabernacle, we should cry out like St. Francis,

"We adore you, O Christ,
here and in all the tabernacles of the world,
and we praise you because by your holy Cross,
you have redeemed the world!"

My good and dear Jesus, I kneel before you asking you most earnestly to engrave upon my heart a deep and lively faith, hope, and charity, with true repentance for my sins and a firm resolve to make amends. As I reflect upon your five wounds, and dwell upon them with deep compassion and grief, I recall, good Jesus, the words the Prophet David spoke long ago concerning yourself: "They pierced my hands and m feet; they have numbered all my bones." *Amen.*

Make me after thine own fashion
Christ's companion in his passion,
all his pain and dying bear

Jesus, may your Cross defend me,
And your Mother's prayer befriend me;
Let me die in your embrace

While my body here decays,
may my soul thy goodness praise,
safe in paradise with thee. Amen.

Fac ut portem Christi mortem passionis fac consortem et plagas recolere
Christe cum sit hinc exire da per Matrem me venire ad palmam vicoriae
Quando corpus morietur fac ut animae donetur paradisi gloria. *Amen*

The Twenty-Second Psalm

David, the shepherd and king, was also a prophet who wrote many songs, called psalms, about his love for God. These psalms became the prayers of the Jewish people. When David's descendent, Jesus Christ, sang the psalms, they became songs of God's love for us. In one song, David sang of his persecutions and suffering, and this psalm became the song of Jesus on the Cross, Who began it by reciting the first line: "My God, my God, why have you forsaken me?"

Let us end our journey together through the Stations of the Cross by praying this Psalm with Jesus, followed by the prayer Holy Mother Church has given us to receive a plenary indulgence.

y God, my God, why hast thou forsaken me? Why art thou so far from helping me, from the words of my groaning?
O my God, I cry by day, but thou dost not answer;
  and by night, but find no rest.

Yet thou art holy,
  enthroned on the praises of Israel.
In thee our fathers trusted;
  they trusted, and thou didst deliver them.
To thee they cried, and were saved;
  in thee they trusted, and were not disappointed.

But I am a worm, and no man;
  scorned by men, and despised by the people.
All who see me mock at me,
  they make mouths at me, they wag their heads;
"He committed his cause to the Lord; let him deliver him,
  let him rescue him, for he delights in him!"

Yet thou art he who took me from the womb;
  thou didst keep me safe upon my mother's breasts.
Upon thee was I cast from my birth,
  and since my mother bore me, thou hast been my God.
Be not far from me, for trouble is near
  and there is none to help.

Many bulls encompass me,
  strong bulls of Bashan surround me;
they open wide their mouths at me,
  like a ravening and roaring lion.

I am poured out like water,
  and all my bones are out of joint;
my heart is like wax,
  it is melted within my breast;
my strength is dried up like a potsherd,
  and my tongue cleaves to my jaws;
  Thou dost lay me in the dust of death.

Yea, dogs are round about me;
  a company of evildoers encircle me;
  they have pierced my hands and feet—

I can count all my bones—
  they stare and gloat over me;
they divide my garments among them,
  and for my raiment they cast lots.

But thou, O Lord, be not far off!
  O thou my help, hasten to my aid!

Deliver my soul from the sword,
  my life from the power of the dog!
Save me from the mouth of the lion,
  my afflicted soul from the horns of the wild oxen!

I will tell of thy name to my brethren;
  in the midst of the congregation I will praise thee:
You who fear the Lord, praise him!
  all you sons of Jacob, glorify him,
  and stand in awe of him, all you sons of Israel!
For he has not despised or abhorred
  the affliction of the afflicted;
and he has not hid his face from him,
  but has heard, when he cried to him.

From thee comes my praise in the great congregation;
  my vows I will pay before those who fear him.
The afflicted shall eat and be satisfied;
  those who seek him shall praise the Lord!
  May your hearts live for ever!

All the ends of the earth shall remember
  and turn to the Lord;
and all the families of the nations
  shall worship before him.
For dominion belongs to the Lord,
  and he rules over the nations.

Yea, to him shall all the proud of the earth bow down;
  before him shall bow all who go down to the dust,
  and he who cannot keep himself alive.
Posterity shall serve him;
  men shall tell of the Lord to the coming generation,
and proclaim his deliverance to a people yet unborn,
  that he has wrought it.